How to Choose a
ROOMMATE

ANDREW MOTE

PAGE PUBLISHING, INC.
Conneaut Lake, PA

First originally published by Page Publishing 2020

ISBN 978-1-64628-143-5 (pbk)
ISBN 978-1-64628-144-2 (digital)

Printed in the United States of America

CONTENTS

Oh, what times we had! Oh, what battles we've had! Some good memories, some bad memories, but all in all, they are times that we will never forget and learn from. Roommates. Let's reflect on the times we had with them. Remember when we had that small get-together, kickbacks, party, gatherings with just a few friends over. But all these people who we never invited seem to just show up and now you got a fun party for the moment. Music, dancing, laughing, smoking, and drinking—such a good time. You go to use the bathroom and awe, damn! Someone just threw up all over the sink, toilet, and floor, so guess who gets to clean it up. Your roommate goes to their room, and there's people having sex in their room, in their bed. Now the party isn't so much fun now. There's a knock at the door, and your roomie say, "That's it, no one else is coming in," and it's the police at the door, telling you about the loud noise. Now, the next morning, another knock at the door, and it's your landlord. A citation and possible eviction notice. All this doesn't look good for the next place you will move to with your name on the lease. Just one of many more horror stories to be told. When the word roommate is said, these are just a few thoughts. Economical: If my rent or mortgage is $1,000 a month, I can save myself 500 extra dollars by getting a roommate along with paying half of the bills and utilities. Comforting: It's nice to come home and have someone to talk to and know that I am not alone so nothing bad happens to me. Fun: We can invite our friends over for parties, social gatherings, study groups, and many more, but usually, when there's good, there's bad. Not so nice to come home to a house with the sink full of dishes, food on the floor, and filthy bathroom. Fun: Those invited friends are smoking in the house and not just cigarettes either. Cigarette burns in the carpet and furniture. Of all your invited guests, there are those who do not like one another, and now there's a physical altercation (and we all know a small fight usually turns into a bigger one), and they're now destroying our whole place. This is only a few escapades, but so many more can happen.

But a roommate, *hmmm*?

Well, here's what I'm going to do for you? I will give you some helpful information that hopefully will alleviate, reduce, and eliminate bad experiences with choosing and having a roommate.

The information provided are things to take into consideration and used when deciding on choosing a roommate. Even though all is not full proof because we all are so very different, these useful tools could help you in deciding if you have a best new friend and angel to live with you, or Satan in disguise. Just use some common sense and good judgment in your decision-making. Good luck and happy readings.

CHAPTER 1

GO WITH WHO YOU KNOW

Most people I know have either a lot of friends or just a few. Friends are nice to have, especially if their good ones. Friends are people we like. We have things in common with, they are there to support you, are there for you in your time of need, to do fun things with and on and on. So wouldn't it be a wise choice to choose this person as a roommate. This is nice because it cuts down on things, like arguing and having disagreements over what to watch on the television, since you probably enjoy the same or similar things to watch. Your friends are more than likely to give you respect when it comes to the things in your residence, like food, clothing or other belongings of yours, as well as giving you privacy. Don't like to be left alone nowadays with all the negative elements out there and bad things going on in today's society?

Well, having a roommate is a benefit (male or female) because, with the criminal mind, there is no line, so if there's more people around, they are less likely to do anything foul around you. Your friends would generally be of the same quality, so when you have people over, everyone will get along and respect the residents and others. But beware and cautious because there is a serious downside to this. You may be saying this sounds really good. I'll just do this. Okay, the downside: When we make friends, we like to keep them, but when someone does you wrong, many things, including your friendship, will go south. Example: Your roommate may take an attraction to your boyfriend or girlfriend, and do something that they might regret (hmm, figure that one out, Einstein). They may borrow money from you, and when it's time to pay you back, there's excuse after excuse. They may use something of yours without your permission that has value to you, and they may lose or break it.

It's nice to have friends to do the fun things together, but we know that when a friend does something seriously wrong to you, most likely the friendship may end. But if you're the "our friendship is more important than that" type, then by all means, go for it. Ask family or friends if they know of anyone that's interested in having or needing a roommate. This way you may not know the person, but in a roundabout way, you do because you're familiar with the person you're asking, and you feel comfortable with who they may refer you to. And if anything bad happens, like if they steal or disappear on you, you have an idea on who to go to and ask to get information on them so they're not like a complete stranger. So be sure that the friend or family member you ask says something good about the person and that they are trustworthy and has good judgment morals and values.

CHAPTER 2

THIS IS OUR PLACE,
NOT FOR EVERYONE ELSE

I t's Friday, which is usually a good day for most—can't wait to get home, kick your shoes off, unwind, and get ready for the weekend. Your boss let you go home early, so you get home unexpected. You walk in and hear your roommate in their room doing the "oochie cuchi." Their bedroom door is open, so you give them respect and privacy and go to the door to close it for them and who do you see—your roommate is doing the nasty with your boyfriend or girlfriend. "How could you do this to me?" Why did this happen?

When I say this is our place, however roommates you have may, you have to let it be known that if there are friends, girlfriends, boyfriends that they are involved with, they cannot be spending the night and stay over constantly. And if you do have them over, make sure everyone is properly dressed because a disaster is waiting to happen because, if you are two female roommates and your boyfriend is over and sees your roomie walking around the house with a thin Tang Top and G-string, the male mind does wander. So it is best to have respect and decency for everyone in the house. Do not let others get comfortable when they come over, thinking it's okay to always go into the refrigerator and help themselves to what they want to eat and drink. Coming over and turning your TV on to watch what they want to watch, bringing their clothes over to wash because you have a washer and a dryer, and they do not want to go to the laundry mat. This is trouble waiting to happen. So what needs to be done is to have a discussion regarding friends and family staying over for the night. Once in a blue moon is fine, but when it starts to become constant, rest assured, problems will arise. And if boyfriends and girlfriends start staying over, there will become a bigger problem because if you have disagreements because of them, we have a tendency to defend the one we're with before others, except for family, I would think.

There has to be an open discussion regarding all these matters and make sure there is a mutual agreement, in writing and signed, with everyone.

CHAPTER 3

SET UP AN INTERVIEW

To put an ad online or a on paper for a roommate is almost like inviting a serial killer in to your residence. If a complete stranger knocks on your door, do you just open to the door and ask, "May I help you?" and then invite them in? Those of us who think safety first would not. So why would you have someone live with you, knowing nothing about them? Not in today's world. It is an unsure way of knowing whom you will be living with. No way of knowing what kind of bad element you will be inviting in, and worse than that, living with. So what do you do?

The Interview

When applying for a new job, what is one of the biggest things you have to go through? An interview. Why not do the same thing with the person you will be living with. The interview does not have to be so in-depth, but make it more personal so that the person who will be living with you will not feel like it's just a business contract. Have some questions ready so when you have your talk, you can determine if this person is worth the time and sacrifice to let into your residence.

When you set up the interview, make it for a time and place that is comfortable for you because you are the one that is taking more of a risk than they are. Do not conduct the interviews at your home. If you have talked to seven or eight people and only decide on one, they now know where you live, what you have in your house, they know your alone because you are still looking, etc., get the picture. Starbucks, Buffalo Wild Wings, just to name a few places, may be good to just sit down and talk but don't give out too much information about you. Keep it simple and to the point. Once they have moved in and you get acquainted with one another, now you can open up about yourself if you feel comfortable. Always be cautious. And if you still feel uncomfortable for the first time, bring a friend with you. Two level heads may make a better judgment than just one. Before the interview, introduce yourself and let them know that if they don't mind, you have a few questions you would like to ask to get to know them better. If they have nothing to hide, then most of the time, the answer of "sure" is what you will get, if not, then you know right away, move on to the next.

Here are a few sample questions to ask:

1) Are you working?

If they are living off unemployment or student loans, this money has an expiration date, meaning there is only so much until it runs out, but a job usually does not unless you quit or get fired, so make sure they have consistent income. And say, "Oh, where do you work and how long have you been there?" If they just started, be cautious, but if they say at least a year, then you should be okay but just don't take their word, verify their income in some way.

2) Are you in the military?

This is great for you. It may not be much, but they will always have a source of income, and women and men in the military are disciplined from training, and most that are usually take pride in themselves and their belongings along with honor and respect. Plus, if they happen to just up and leave or do any damage to your residence, they are property of the military andwould more than likely be reprimanded in some fashion so I would advise to contact the tenants Commanding Officer or someone of rank on whichever military installation they may be stationed and inform them of your situation.

3) Do you have kids?

A lot of people love kids, but not all. If you love your quiet time, are in school and study quite a bit, then someone with kids may not be for you. We all have our right to have a choice, and by all means, you are not portraying hate on kids by saying no thank you, but it is your choice. Do not personally tell someone thanks but no thanks, because someone with kids just may take it personal. Anyone who has kids knows that, even if you have them on certain days of the week or month, things change. So if you are okay with this, then tell them that this is okay.

4) Trick question.

"Do you do drugs?" I say this because most that do drugs will not say anything, and you have to find out the hard way. Can you imagine coming home to find the DEA in your residence and your roommate in handcuffs? And what will be your typical answer? "I didn't know he/she was selling drugs." Typical cop answer (or thought), "Sure you didn't." So the trick question would be to say, "Do you do drugs because I do occasionally, so if you have a problem with it let me know" and see what the response is? If they tell you that they do drugs also, now you know up front and can save yourself a lot of headache and tell them, "Okay, cool." Finish the interview but make it short; don't finish the rest of the questions, and tell them you will call them and let them know on your decision. And when they call you, and they will, just tell them you found someone else and thank them for their time. Now, if you tell them you do drugs and they say they do not and start to get up to leave, just tell them you were testing them to see if they did and be honest in saying that you do not. Most people will understand when you explain to them why you said that, and would be sympathetic with your reasoning.

5) Can you cook?

Those who know how to cook usually clean up after themselves, which means your place will be clean.

What do they like to do for fun?
What kind of music do you like?
Where did you grow up?
Are you a homebody, or do you like to go out and party?
What are your goals in life?
And so on?

CHAPTER 4

GET IT IN WRITING

So many of us have been duped, hoodwinked, hornswoggled, conned by taking someone's word and not having anything in writing. So my advice is to make up a contract, does not have to be anything elaborate, and a contract does not have to have all the fancy does and don'ts on it. You can make it up yourself with just a few simple things. For example: This is a six-month agreement. At the end of the six-month period, I (your name) will decide if occupant (roommate's name) will continue to stay for another six months. If so, sign and date (your name) on a specified area, and they will do the same. If not, have an area also specified to sign and date and have an additional line for the reasons why their occupancy will be terminated. And specify a time frame they have to vacate their property from your premises. This does not have to be for six months. It's your contract, so you make up the time frame.

If there is constant partying of drug use in your residence, put those stipulations in the contract so that, by your decision, could be cause for immediate termination of contract and that said occupant (name) has seventy-two hours to remove property and vacate premises. If they happen to take a vacation for a week or two, make sure they keep in contact with you by leaving a message by phone, text, or email so that you know they just did not up and leave and will not be returning. And if the time frame has been three weeks since you have seen them, many of us take the word of others to heart and believe what they say, and because they did not have anything in writing, they lose out if they are taken to court. Also, if they have a car, notate the license plate number and put it somewhere for later. Again, just in case. Main point: Put your mutual agreements in black and white, with both of your names and signatures, along with the date. "Make sure once everyone has signed, take it to get notarized and save it on your computer or phone for future reference". In some kind of way of fashion, take a picture of your new roommate and send it to someone close to you. This way if anything at all ever happens to you, a face is now recognizable for whatever reason.

CHAPTER 5

HAVE THEM FILL OUT
A PRE-APPLICATION

S ounds foolish, I know, but we're talking about a lot of things at stake? Your home and the property inside. Your safety as well as the neighbors. Why risk this? The pre-application just has a few minor things for you to gain some general information about your maybe-future roommate.

Last name

First name

Address

Date of birth

Last two places of employment

Now that you have their names and addresses, which is good to have for future reference and in case anything bad happens down the road, here is what you do with this tidbit of information.

As soon as you get back to your place, or any place with internet access, go on to a computer and run a background check. I know, it may seem underhanded to pry into someone's life and history, but if it's at the cost of having you and your property stolen, as well as possibly your identity, then you will have no problem with it. How about someone with an extensive criminal history, someone who has done time for rape, attempted sexual assault, burglary, drugs, attempted murder. I would say it is worth the time and effort. And let's be honest, your life can depend on it. These are just a few sites that are very useful in obtaining background information on individuals, but are well worth the money: *sentrylink.com, USSearch.com, instantcheckmate.com, Beenverified.com, truthfinder.com, Intelius.com, peoplefinders.com.*

To make sure you have the right individual, make sure you match up the last name, first name with things like their age or address. This way you know you will have the right person.

CHAPTER 6

HOW ABOUT SOMEONE OLDER?

This sounds great. Our elders are the ones who teach us, guide us, point us in the right direction, and pave the way for us—our leaders of the world. So yes, to be around someone older definitely has its advantages, but I would not feel right about saying all the positives without knowing some negatives. Elders run our corporations, lead our countries, run our organizations, and set our laws. On the other side, young criminals get caught; older criminals are on the run longer. Point being: Older people are more devious in their plots, so if you don't know who you're going to be living with, pay attention to this. If you are a woman and decide to choose an older male for a roommate, he may have an underlying interest in either being around you or your girlfriends. If you are a woman and choose to have an older woman as a roommate, she sees you as younger. Her thoughts are of you as a daughter figure, meaning, she likes to take control and tell you and your friends what to do because since she feels she's older, "I should get the bigger room. Your friends need to be out by midnight." I would not feel right about saying all the positives without the negatives, so here we go.

Positives:

> More mature.
> Stable income.
> Wealth of information.
> Better at handling conflict and drama.

Negatives:

> Older person hanging around with youth—weird.
> Not into partying and crowds.
> Does not like a lot of noise.
> Sticker for rules.

The majority of people usually hangs around and associate themselves with people in their own age range because we have more things in common. Conversations we can both understand and relate to, but our choices are what make us unique, so if your instincts tell you "I'm okay with him or her," then go with what you feel.

CHAPTER 7

ALWAYS STAY OBSERVANT

You've had a roommate now for seven months, do not seem to have a job and always have loads of money. If they are always in and out for short periods of time, has two or more cell phones and people are always coming and going, trust me, they are not just friends. Start looking at that contract you had them signed and highlight "drug dealing is strictly prohibited and is in violation of contract which is cause for forty-eight to seventy-two eviction of premises." If they are late more than one time with the rent, it is cause for a concern. Let them know that if it's late one more time, you have to look at the agreement that they signed about late rent. If you start to notice they do not clean after themselves, do not clean the kitchen or bathroom. It's a sign of someone that is not very tidy and expects you to clean all the time. Tell them right from the start about cleaning habits because, if you do it on occasion, they will think you are going to do it all the time, so no babysitting. Make sure to add these stipulations in the contract so there's not debating on responsibilities.

Make it a habit of always, of always, checking the place before you leave and when you get home, like are all the doors and windows locked? Turn off utilities that are not needed, like lights, air conditioner, heater, cable boxes, etc. You're taking on a roommate to save money, not throw it away.

People may not want to admit it, but many are curious by nature, or should I say the word, nosey. I would suggest getting a lock for your bedroom door. Put all your valuables in your room, like jewelry, iPad, laptops, tools, and cameras, anything that is small but of value. If you do not put a lock on your door, then purchase a small webcam that monitors your bedroom and point it at your door. Make sure your camera is not just monitoring but recording so you can use it as proof as to why your roommate, or anyone else for the matter, entered your room. Locked or unlocked.

Another safe place to put your belongings would be in your car. The first thing we all do when we get out of our vehicles is to lock the doors. It's an automatic instinct, so if you lock your valuables in your car, they are secure. Just make sure they are not in plain sight and are in the trunk of your car or in the glove box.

So many things to consider, and there is never a foolproof way to choose the perfect roommate, but in doing so, look at yourself as well. Think long and hard about the pros and cons of your choice. Ask yourself, *A m I a loner and just don't want to be around someone all the time? Am I so nitpicky that I would chase them away?* I don't pick up after myself, and my place is usually a mess? Having a roommate goes both ways, and that's why talking about both of your good points and bad points would help in deciding if the two, or more, of you would get along living together.

So, in the end, know for sure if this is what you want to do. Make a list of the pros and cons, and which one outweighs the other. Ask family and friends what they think. Is there other option I may want to explore?

Having a roommate can give you memories that you looked back and were happy about, laughed at, gained knowledge from, or an experience you will never go through again, made you file for bankruptcy, and had a terrible physical experience that scarred you emotionally for life. We want all the good and none of the bad, so I truly hope this helps you in making the best choices possible in how to choose a roommate.

These are my helpful hints with little things that go along with saving money and life choices.

Try not to go into convenience stores between the hours of 2:00 am and 5:00 am. These are prime times when there are no customers, and these stores are likely to get robbed, so don't be caught in the middle of this. Instead, go to a major store like

Walmart, Ralph's, Smiths, Raleys. Stores that are twenty-four hours. They are always well lit, and there are customers and employees around, even at this time of the morning.

If you are on a budget and eat quite a bit of takeout, when you order your food, you are given packets of ketchup, soy sauce, salt, pepper, napkins, forks and spoons. When you are given these items, ask for extras and start stacking them away. That way you do not have to go to the store and purchase these goods. This would mainly be for someone young and in college, not much income, you hit hard times and are struggling, or your just very frugal.

Hangover cure:

Drink 8 ounces of Gatorade, 8 ounces of V8, and an 8 ounces glass of water, Alka-Seltzer. And no, you do not mix them all together, consume them separately. Would you rather have the nasty taste for a few minutes or the nauseating feeling and headache all day? If you are going to have a party, keep these goods ready and available. Trust me. It works. One hour and *wala*!

Keep at least two liters of club soda around. Soda water is an automatic stain lifter. Got a stain on your shirt or pants? Immediately pour club soda on it and do not rub it, dab the stain. Once you dab it, pour a little laundry detergent on the stain and a little more club soda on it, and let it sit for approximately thirty minutes, then wash it with regular clothing. And if you happen to be out on the town, seltzer water also works. This also works with carpeting. Once you dab the carpeting, you can pour a little laundry detergent on your carpet to also remove the stain, but make sure the detergent *does not* have bleach in it or your carpet will now have a white bleach stain.

To make your teeth whiter when brushing your teeth, put the regular amount of toothpaste on your toothbrush and pour some hydrogen peroxide on the bristles. And for even brighter teeth, sprinkle some baking soda on the bristles, pour hydrogen peroxide as well, and then apply the toothpaste. Much of the toothpaste now being sold contains peroxide and baking soda, all you are doing is using more of a concentrated version, and when you are done brushing your teeth, pour more peroxide on the bristles of your toothbrush to help keep it clean from buildup of germs. Most of us just rinse our toothbrushes with water and do not sterilize. Our mouths are full of germs, so it would be smart to sterilize your toothbrush.

If you're having a party, get-together, kickback, people over, make sure one of you stays sober. If you have people over for gatherings, something bad usually happens. And it does not have to be something severely bad, but things like the music is too loud, glasses being broke, drinks spilled on the carpet, to name just a few. The sober roommate can handle these and the unforeseeable problems and take care of them. If the music is too loud and the police arrive, they do not want to talk to someone who is inebriated, so one of you has to have the level head. That webcam you set up in your room? Take it out, lock your door, and set it up somewhere in the house where everyone is mostly congregating. If something gets broken, stolen, and a fight happens, you have it recorded for evidence to fall back on later. So if the drunk says, "I didn't break that table" because they were too drunk to remember, you have it on video. Keynote: Post a couple small notes that state, "these premises are under audio and video recording," and take a picture of them with your cell phone. That way, no one can say you were producing illegal recordings. Liability can fall on you if someone gets drunk in your residence, drives off, and kills either themselves or someone else, so play it smart and have a key man at the party. The key man is posted at the door, and like when people used to take your coat, he takes your keys and gives you a paper with a number to show which keys are yours when you leave. If you are noticeably drunk, you do not get keys back. Be courteous and give your neighbors a heads up that you will be having people over. Give them your number in case things get too loud or someone happens to climb in their backyard.

Inquiries:
Email-illdowhatican4u@yahoo.com
Facebook-https://www.facebook.com/HowToChooseaRoommate/
Twitter-@aawwwyeah

ABOUT THE AUTHOR

Andrew Mote has an immeasurable knack for writing, as well as his love for acting and his kids. Action, thrillers, and comedy are his strong points, but his love for writing is extreme. He has a long background of evaluating the psyche of others, teaching, and customer service. Well known from his colleagues of having a big heart for anyone and anything good and positive, and his writing is intended to give others helpful information to open the eyes and mind to all life's discrepancies in an effort to go around them instead of through them. Why suffer pain when you don't have to? He is an inventor with an artistic mind and a passion to give and make as many, in and out of his circle, better human beings. His, and all children, are first and foremost in life, and an outlook of whatever we strive to achieve in life, some of that effort should be put to saving, helping, or contributing into making the children of our world better. Andrew has been around thousands of personalities and characteristics throughout his life, young and old, which helps to discover the unending differences of people in our world. He makes every attempt to put his readers in touch with what is actually happening when they are reading. If you can put yourself in a "that-could-happen-to-me" situation, then you are grasping exactly what Andrew is trying to portray. His time of having roommates, when in college and out, as well as talking with others who were in similar situations, was put in this book to help the many that had to pay a heavy sacrifice when they did not do their homework when choosing a roommate.

Printed in the USA
CPSIA information can be obtained
at www.ICGtesting.com
CBHW031200090324
5168CB00009B/398